D0432228

# THE OLYMPICS
# EVENTS

## Moira Butterfield

SEA-TO-SEA

*Mankato  Collingwood  London*

This edition first published in 2012 by

Sea-to-Sea Publications
Distributed by Black Rabbit Books
P.O. Box 3263, Mankato, Minnesota 56002

Published by arrangement with the Watts
Publishing Group Ltd, London.

Library of Congress Cataloging-in-Publication Data

Butterfield, Moira, 1960-
 The Olympics: Events / by Moira Butterfield.
   p. cm. -- (The Olympics)
 Includes index.
 ISBN 978-1-59771-321-4 (library binding)
 1. Olympics--Juvenile literature. I. Title.
 GV721.53.B878 2012
 796.48--dc22

                              2011006465


 Series editor: Sarah Ridley
 Editor in chief: John C. Miles
 Designer: Jason Billin
 Art director: Jonathan Hair
 Picture research: Diana Morris

 Picture credits: Allsport/Getty Images: 26. Robert Beck/Sports Illustrated/Getty Images: 11b.
Alessandro dell Bella/epa/Corbis: 22c. Greg Breloer/Corbis: 5. Mark Dadswell/Getty Images: 10. Fred
Dufour/AFP/Getty Images: 24t. Don Emmert/AFP/Getty Images: 24b. Chris Faytok/Star Ledger/Corbis:
22b. Julian Finney/Getty Images: 27. Guo Lei/Xinhua Press/Corbis: 21. Julian Herbert/Getty Images: 12,
13. Jo Yong-Hak/Reuters/Corbis: 16b. Jung Keon-Je/AFP/Getty Images: 19t. Streeter Lecka/Getty
Images: 3, 18. Liu Dawei/Xinhua/Corbis: 8. Alex Livesey/Getty Images: 28. Kat Nietfeld/epa/Corbis: 9.
Professional Sport/Topfoto: 15t, 19c. Quinn Rooney/Getty Images: 11t, 14. Sampics/Corbis: 17. Erich
Schlegel/Dallas Morning News/Corbis: 16c. Carl de Souza/AFP/Getty Images: 15c. Jamie Squire/Getty
Images: front cover. Matthew Stockman/Getty Images: 29. Al Tielemans/Sports Illustrated/Getty
Images: 7. Ullsteinbild/Topfoto: 6, 20. Manan Vatsyayana/AFP/Getty Images: 25. Xu
Jiajun/Xinhua/Corbis: 23.

Every attempt has been made to clear copyright. Should there be any inadvertent omission please apply to
the publisher for rectification.

February 2011
RD/6000006415/001

## Note to parents and teachers

Every effort has been made by the Publishers to ensure that the web sites in this book
are suitable for children, that they are of the highest educational value, and that they
contain no inappropriate or offensive material. However, because of the nature of the
Internet, it is impossible to guarantee that the contents of these sites will not be altered.
We strongly advise that Internet access is supervised by a responsible adult.

# CONTENTS

The Summer Olympic Games are held every four years, and showcase the fastest, strongest, and most skilled sportspeople on the planet. The world's swiftest runners compete in the track events, held in and around the Olympic Stadium.

The fastest races—the 100 meters (m), 200 m, and 400 m—are called sprints. They are over in just a few exciting seconds. The runners start from blocks and must stay in eight numbered lanes marked on the track. Sensors are installed in the starting gun and the blocks, and if they detect that a runner has started less than 0.1 seconds after the gun is fired, it counts as a false start. To win, runners must get their torso (the body between the head to waist) across the line first.

### Middle- and Long-Distance Events
The 800 m and 1,500 m are called "middle-distance" races. The 5,000 m and 10,000 m are called "long-distance" races. The athletes begin a race spread across

Jamaican record-breaker Usain Bolt prepares himself before the final of the Beijing 100 m sprint in 2008.

staggered lanes—the ones in the outer lanes begin farther forward to compensate for the bends in the track. Then, after a certain distance, all the competitors are allowed to bunch together in one lane. The Olympic Stadium track is 400 m long, so in the longer events, the athletes run around again and again.

## Hurdles, Steeplechases, and Relays

Hurdlers and steeplechasers must jump hurdles as they race. Some of the steeplechase hurdles have pools of water in front of them, and landing in the water will slow down an athlete, so the steeplechasers need to clear the hurdle as well as the pool. Track relay events have four runners in a team. Each one takes a turn running with a baton. They must hand the baton over to the next athlete in a changeover box 20 m in length marked on the track, but if they fumble, the handover race will be lost.

○ In track relay events, the athletes must get the baton handover technique perfect.

### Amazing Olympics

In the Paralympics, there are different track-event categories including wheelchair races and events for runners with amputated limbs or visual impairment.

### Olympic Facts and Stats

All track races are run counterclockwise. Each race can have one false start, and then anyone who makes a false start after that is disqualified (banned from the race).

The longest Olympic running race is the marathon, at more than 26 miles (42 km). It is run on roads outside the Olympic Stadium.

The longest Olympic track race of all is the 31-mile (50-km) men's walk.

# EVENTS

Field events are held in the middle of the Olympic Stadium. They include jumping competitions, throwing events, and combined events, which include a combination of sports such as throwing, jumping, and running.

The jumping events include the high jump, long jump, triple jump, and pole vault. The high jumpers must clear a bar that is gradually raised higher during the competition. The pole vaulters sprint toward the high bar, plant their pole, and try to sail over the bar. If the high jumpers or pole vaulters knock the bar off three times at the same height, they are out of the competition. The long jumpers sprint along a runway and leap over a sandpit from the front of a takeoff board. If their takeoff foot goes over the front of the board, the judges wave a red flag and the jump doesn't count. The triple jumpers take a long hop and a step before they jump over the sandpit.

## Throwing Events

The throwing events include the discus, hammer, shot put, and javelin. These sports are among the oldest in Olympic history. The ancient Greeks, who invented the Olympic Games in

◁ Australian Steve Hooker clears the bar on his way to winning the pole vault gold medal at Beijing in 2008.

776 B.C.E., threw spears and the discus in their competitions. When they are throwing, the competitors must stay inside a specifically marked area.

## Combined Events

The Olympic combined events are the decathlon for men, the heptathlon for women, and the modern pentathlon. Decathletes compete in ten different track and field sports in two days. The overall winner is the athlete with the most points. The heptathletes try seven events over two days, and the modern pentathlon competitors have just one day to combine a 3-km-cross-country run with shooting, fencing, swimming, and horseback riding events.

▶ Aksana Miankova from Belarus wins the Beijing Olympics women's hammer gold medal with a new Olympic-record distance of 76.34 m (about 250.5 feet).

### Olympic Facts and Stats

Pole-vaulting competitions, where the athletes vaulted over live bulls, were held in ancient Greece and Crete.

Pole vaulters used to be able to climb up their poles as they jumped, but this is now against the rules.

Throwing equipment, such as shot puts, discus, and hammers, is heavier for the men's events than for the women's.

Ancient Greek Olympic long jumpers carried weights in their hands as they jumped. This helped propel them forward, so they may have jumped farther than today's athletes.

Summer Olympic aquatic events take place in a custom-built swimming arena. The competitions include swimming, diving, synchronized swimming, and water polo.

Swimmers race in eight lanes in a pool 165 feet (50 m) in length. There are 34 different events for men and women, split into different swimming techniques—breaststroke, butterfly, backstroke, and freestyle (crawl), the fastest swimming style. At the end of each lane is an electronic pad swimmers must touch as they turn or finish, to register their time. Competitors must be physically fit with great stamina because they need to qualify through heats and semifinals to earn the chance to compete for a medal in a final. A brand new swimming event was introduced in 2008, a marathon 10-km open-water swim, with the competitors swimming outdoors in a lake.

🔽 American Michael Phelps, one of the all-time great Olympians, powers down the pool.

**Amazing Olympics**

In Paralympic swimming, there are different event categories, including races for the blind, physically disabled, and mentally impaired.

## Diving Events

There are events for single divers and synchronized diving competitions. There are several different types of dives, including forward and backward dives, twisting dives, and even a dive that begins with a handstand. Some events take place on the springboard, others take place on a high-dive platform. Judges score the dives out of ten.

△ In the synchronized dives, the two divers try to dive in perfect time with each other.

## Synchronized Swimming and Water Polo

There are team and individual womens' synchronized swimming events. Judges score the swimmers on technical moves and artistic performance set to music. There are 20 basic positions and some of them are performed completely underwater. Water polo is very noisy and the players move fast. Teams of seven play in a swimming pool inside an area marked with floating buoys and goals. They are only allowed to use one hand to throw the waterproof ball into the goal in order to score.

▽ A goalkeeper looks on anxiously as a shot comes in during the Beijing water polo competition.

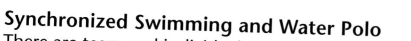

### Olympic Facts and Stats

Open-water marathon swimmers can be penalized just like players in other team sports. They get a yellow card for bad behavior, followed by a red card, which disqualifies them.

The synchronized swimming pool has underwater speakers, so the performers can hear the music underwater.

Any Olympic swimmer who makes a false start is immediately disqualified.

Blind Paralympic swimmers have a "tapper." This is a person who taps them with a pole to let them know they are nearing the end of the pool.

# EVENTS

The Olympic Equestrian (riding) program includes three different types of event—show-jumping, eventing, and dressage. Men and women compete together in individual and team competitions.

At the Olympic show-jumping arena there are individual and team events. The horses must ride around a course laid out with jumping fences, gates, and water jumps. Some of the fences are in rows of two or three. The riders pick up penalty points if they knock down fence poles, refuse to jump, put a hoof in a water jump, go the wrong way, or take too long. Both the riders and the horses have to keep calm and be resourceful to cope with the challenges.

▽ A show-jumper clears a jump in the 2008 Olympic show-jumping arena.

○ In dressage, a rider whose horse looks happy and alert gets more points than one whose horse looks tense.

## Dressage

The dressage event is a very precise display of horsemanship. It's like a complicated dance, designed to demonstrate how good a horse is at responding to its rider's commands. It has to go through a series of set movements including cantering, trotting, and different types of walk. Judges watch carefully and mark each performance out of ten, for technique and elegance.

## Eventing

In the eventing competition, the riders take part in four events over three days—dressage, cross-country, and two rounds of show-jumping. At 3.75 miles (6 km) long, the cross-country course is one of the toughest challenges in the entire Summer Olympics, with water-filled ditches, streams, and high fences to jump at a gallop. The horses must be strong and the riders fearless, but they also need to be able to do the precise movements of dressage.

## Amazing Olympics

Horses are flown to the Olympic host city in passenger jets, in specially adapted areas of the airplane hold. Trained "flight grooms" look after the animals during the flights.

## Olympic Facts and Stats

Olympic horses are tested for illegal performance-enhancing drugs, just like human athletes.

Athletes in the modern pentathlon are loaned a horse for their show-jumping round and have just 20 minutes to get to know the animal.

The word *dressage* comes from the French *dresser*, which means "to train." The technique was once used for training cavalry horses in the army.

There were horse-drawn chariot races at the ancient Greek Olympics.

There are four different Olympic cycling categories—track cycling, road racing, mountain biking, and BMX racing. The track cycling takes place in a custom-built velodrome—an arena with an oval-shaped, sloped wooden racetrack.

There are ten different track cycling competitions for men and women. The fastest races are the sprints, where riders play a slow-cycling game of cat and mouse for two laps and then explode at speeds up to 60 mph (96 km/h) in the final lap, trying to catch one another by surprise. In the team cycling events, you will see riders in a team taking turns riding in front, trying to outwit their opponents. The longest and most complicated team race is the Madison. In this race, teams of two riders take turns riding over a marathon 200 laps, winning points for their position every 20 laps.

## Amazing Olympics

The velodrome track has lines on it. The red line is for overtaking, the black line shows the shortest route, and the blue line marks where team cyclists can take a break.

◀ Cyclists in the Olympic velodrome power around the track's banked (sloped) sides.

Mountain bikes have to be tough to survive a rugged cross-country race.

## Road and Cross-Country Events

Road cyclists race over a course of 148.5 miles (239 km) for men or 74.5 miles (120 km) for women, or they take part in time trials against the clock. It usually takes about six hours for the men to complete the road race, and between three and four hours for the women. Meanwhile the mountain bikers are tested on a tough cross-country course, racing one another or by doing time trials over a rough and hilly track. They "bunny-hop" (jump the bike) over branches, rocks, and streams, or get off the bike and run with it over the steepest parts of the course.

## BMX

An exciting new Olympic sport, BMX bike racing, was introduced at the Beijing Olympics in 2008. Eight riders race over a dirt track littered with jumps, bumps, and tight corners. They fly through the air, launching themselves off of the obstacles as they try to overtake their opponents. Each race lasts for just 40 seconds of fast and furious action.

In BMX racing, the riders must race while coping with sharp turns and jumps on the course.

### Olympic Facts and Stats

Olympic mountain bikers have to carry their own toolkit, in case they need to make quick repairs during races.

At the first modern Olympic Games ever, held in Greece in 1896, just six riders competed in the cycling road race.

In the Keirin track race, the cyclists ride behind a motorcycle, which gradually speeds up in front of them.

The cycling sprinters are only timed over the last 656 feet (200 m) of their race.

# SHOOTING

Target shooting events at the Summer Olympics include competitions using air guns, pistols, rifles, or arrows. In the Winter Olympics, the biathlon combines cross-country skiing with rifle shooting.

There are 15 gun-shooting events for men and women, using various different pistols or rifles. In some of the competitions, the shooters aim at electronic targets marked with ten circles, each one scoring differently. They must concentrate hard to fire a set number of shots in a limited time. The fastest firers are in the rapid-fire pistol events, where the competitors have just a few seconds to fire at a row of five targets. In skeet and trap shooting the shooters aim at saucer-shaped targets shot into the air by a machine. The competitors have to have very fast reactions to hit the disks as they speed across the sky.

## Archery Events

In the archery competitions, the target is 4 feet (1.22 m wide), but looks tiny to an archer standing 230 feet (70 m) away— about the same size as a thumbtack held at arm's length. The target has ten rings, with a bull's-eye 4.8 inches (12.2 cm) wide.

○ Competitors in trap shooting wear padded clothing to protect them from the recoil of the gun.

○ Three South Korean women archers at a media event demonstrate the strength needed to draw an Olympic bow.

Green and red lights tell them when they can shoot and when their time is up, and they have 15 seconds to load an arrow, aim, and fire.

## Shooting from Skis

In the Winter Olympics biathlon events, competitors must complete a tough cross-country ski race, carrying a rifle on their back, before they reach the shooting range. There they must drop their ski poles and take five shots at a target 165 feet (50 m) away. They must do their best to get their heart rate down after the skiing, to give themselves a better chance to shoot accurately. They do this by deep breathing and concentrating hard. If a skier misses a target, minutes are added on to their overall race time. The winner is the competitor who finishes in the shortest time.

A competitor in the Winter Olympics biathlon takes aim through a high-power telescopic sight.

### Olympic Facts and Stats

Shooting and archery competitors have to qualify through different rounds to get to medal finals.

Biathlon ski rifles have special mechanisms attached to the end to stop them from getting blocked with snow.

The string of an Olympic archery bow is stronger than steel.

Olympic archers must bring their own arrows, with their name written on each one.

# SPORTS

Summer Olympic combat sports include boxing, fencing, judo, tae kwon do, and wrestling. They are contested with knockout bouts between two opponents, with the winner going through to another round or winning a medal.

The boxing events are organized by weight categories—so the heaviest or lightest people fight against each other. Judges keep a score as they watch the fight, and the winner either has the highest score at the end of four rounds, or knocks out his opponent. There are two different types of Olympic wrestling— freestyle and Greco-Roman. Wrestling and boxing were part of the ancient Olympics but were much more violent and could even result in death.

## Amazing Olympics

Paralympic combat sports include judo for the visually impaired and wheelchair fencing. With the wheelchairs fixed to the floor, the fencers concentrate solely on swordplay.

◀ Wrestling was one of the original contests at the ancient Olympic Games.

◗ Fists and feet fly as the competitors try to land scoring blows in tae kwon do.

## Judo

Judo contestants fight on a foam mat, wearing loose-fitting judo uniforms called "judogi." A referee and two judges watch as each contestant tries to score an "ippon," the judo version of a knockout, by throwing his opponent onto his back. In tae kwon do, the fighters wear helmets and padding, and their sport is scored by the number of jabs, punches, and kicks they land. Contestants shout a loud cry, a "kiap," every time they try a move.

## Fencing

Olympic fencers use three different types of sword—the foil, epee, or saber. They all have different kinds of handle and different fighting rules. Before each bout the fighters salute each other with their swords. Then a referee shouts, "On guard!" and the bout begins. The fighters must stay inside an area called the "piste," trying to touch each other with the tips of their swords.

◗ The tips of the fencing swords are wired electronically to register a hit when they touch.

### Olympic Facts and Stats

In ancient Greece, any illegal wrestling moves were punished with a whipping from the referee.

Olympic boxers are not allowed to have beards.

In 2012, there will be boxing events for women for the first time in Olympic history.

During fights, judo referees shout "begin" and "finish" in Japanese, while tae kwon do referees shout the same commands in Korean. These countries are where the sports began.

There are many team sport events at the Summer Olympics and the Paralympics. They include well-known sports such as soccer and basketball, and more unusual sports such as beach volleyball and handball.

In Olympic basketball, teams try to score as many baskets as possible against each other, in a timed game. The teams play each other in groups; then the top teams go on to play quarterfinals, semifinals, and finals. Basketball's biggest superstars take part and the games always draw big crowds and millions of TV viewers around the world. Paralympic wheelchair basketball moves fast and is exciting to watch, too. The players use extra-tough titanium wheelchairs designed to cope with the rough and tumble of the game.

### Soccer

Olympic soccer teams are allowed three professional players out of 11. At the 2012 London Olympics, the games will be held in famous soccer stadiums around the UK such as

○ Sports superstar Kobe Bryant finds the basket for the USA basketball team.

Old Trafford, home of Manchester United, and Hampden Park, home of the Scottish soccer team. The Paralympics have five-a-side and seven-a-side soccer, and the ball has a bell fitted inside it to make a sound visually impaired players can hear.

## Handball and Volleyball

In Olympic handball, teams try to score by throwing a ball at a goal. The best attacking players know how to punch the ball to make it spin and bounce in unexpected directions, to fool the goalie. In volleyball and beach volleyball, players use their fists to knock the ball back and forth over a net, trying to keep it going, the way tennis players do. Beach volleyball is played on sand, which makes it harder for players to move around but produces spectacular shots and saves, because the players don't mind falling on the soft sand.

🔵 The beach volleyball court is filled with sand to replicate beach conditions.

**Amazing Olympics**

A new team sport, seven-a-side rugby for men and women, will be part of the Rio De Janeiro Olympics in 2016.

### Olympic Facts and Stats

Paralympic players take part in sitting volleyball, using only their upper bodies to reach the ball.

At the London Olympics in 2012, the beach volleyball competition will be held on a fake beach at Horseguards Parade in Whitehall, central London.

One of the greatest Olympic team medal runs ever was in field hockey, when the Indian team won every gold medal in men's hockey between 1928 and 1956.

In Paralympic soccer for the visually impaired, all the players wear eye masks, to make sure that nobody can see better than anybody else.

# SPORTS

**Badminton, tennis, and table tennis are all part of the Summer Olympics. They are played in individual or team competitions.**

Tennis includes men's and women's singles and doubles, played in knockout competitions. At the 2012 London Olympics the competitions will be played on the world-famous grass courts of Wimbledon. The world's top-ranking players qualify to take part, and some of the greatest players ever have won Olympic gold, including Rafael Nadal (men's singles champion 2008) and Venus Williams (2000 ladies singles champion and 2008 doubles champion with her sister Serena). Tennis is played at the Paralympics, too, in wheelchair events.

## Badminton

Badminton has men's and women's singles and doubles competitions. It is played on an indoor court with a net higher than a standard tennis net, lightweight rackets, and a shuttlecock made of bird feathers. It first became an Olympic sport in 1992, and so far Asian countries have

◢ Spain's Rafael Nadal keeps his eye on the ball en route to the 2008 Olympic men's tennis gold medal.

◀ China's Lin Dan, men's badminton gold medalist, leaps to smash the shuttlecock.

been the most successful. China does extremely well at badminton, with a record 30 medals, 11 of them gold.

## Table Tennis

Men and women play singles and team events in Olympic table-tennis competitions. The sport is very fast and needs good agility, quick reflexes, and great hand-eye coordination. The best players use different techniques to make the ball spin, so it shoots in surprising ways as it bounces. They use wooden bats with a rubber covering, which they glue on only minutes before a match, to ensure the very best bat performance.

### Amazing Olympics

All Olympic sports have their own pictogram—a picture symbol used to represent them on posters and signs at the Games.

◓ Most of the best Olympic table tennis players are from Asian countries, where they are sports superstars.

### Olympic Facts and Stats

The first tennis gold medalist ever was an Irish student who won the men's event in Athens in 1896. He had come to watch the Olympics, and only decided to enter after he arrived.

Tennis players who win at the Olympics get points toward their world ranking, helping them to qualify for other competitions around the world.

Table tennis is also called ping-pong or whiff-whaff. It is a Paralympic wheelchair event.

Table tennis began in the 1800s, when wealthy people played it after formal dinner, using champagne corks as balls and cigar boxes as bats.

# BOAT SPORTS

Rowing, canoeing, and sailing take place on lakes or on the coast of the Summer Olympic host country.

○ Team Australia rowing coxless four at Beijing in 2008.

The Olympic rowing course is set out in a lake, with six lanes marked by buoys on the water. There are 14 different rowing events for men and women, using different-sized boats. Crews are either singles, pairs, fours, or eights. They must be physically fit with loads of stamina to keep going and speed up toward the end of the race. In sculling events each rower has two oars. In sweep races each rower has one oar. The biggest boats are for the eights—eight rowers and a coxswain, who shouts at the rowers to help them keep their rhythm and encourage them to keep trying.

## Sailing Events

There are ten sailing events for men and women, in different boat classes (types of boat). These include dinghies, keelboats (sailing boats), multihulls (boats with more than one hull, such as catamarans), and windsurfers. The competitors sail around a course marked with buoys.

◁ Great Britain's Ben Ainslie wins gold for the fourth time in the Finn Olympic sailing class in Beijing.

They take part in several rounds, earning points for their position as they cross the finishing line. The winner earns the least points overall. The sailors need skill and strength to get around the course, setting their sails to get the maximum speed and power from the wind.

## Canoeing Events

There are two types of canoe event at the Olympics—slalom and sprint. A slalom competition is a timed run down a rough, swirling, white-water course with obstacles, steep drops, and fast currents. There are up to 25 gates to get through, but touching or missing out a gate incurs time penalties. The sprint canoeists race in lanes across calm water, at 200 m, 500 m, or 1,000 m. Some canoeists compete in kayaks, sitting down in the boat and using a paddle with a blade on both sides. Others compete in a canoe, kneeling and using a paddle that has a blade on one side.

**Amazing Olympics**

At the London 2012 Olympics, the sailing will be held off the coast of Dorset. The canoeing will be held in Hertfordshire, and the rowing in Buckinghamshire.

▶ The slalom doubles requires great strength, skill, and teamwork to avoid touching the gates.

### Olympic Facts and Stats

Rowing is the only sport where the competitors cross the line backward.

Coxswains are weighed before they race. If they are lighter than other coxswains in the competition, the judges will add weights to their boat to make the competition more fair.

At the Athens Olympics in 1906, there was a rowing race with 17-man crews.

Olympic windsurfers must all use the same brand of windsurfing equipment, chosen by the IOC, to make sure the competition is fair.

# TECHNIQUE

**Gymnastics and weightlifting are both Olympic categories that demand superb fitness and require many hours of highly focused training to get the technique exactly right.**

Artistic gymnastics is a category of events using apparatus or a floor mat, which includes bars, rings, a vault, or a pommel horse. Tremendous body strength and amazing balance are needed to use them. In the floor exercises, competitors have 70 seconds to combine a sequence of jumps, somersaults, and twists, which are scored by the judges. In rhythmic gymnastics, competitors perform floor routines to music using equipment, which could be a hoop, ribbon, ball, rope, or club. Judges watch all the performances and score them on technique, difficulty, and style. Any slight error could end a medal chance.

◀ Romania's Nadia Comãneci performs a routine at Montreal in 1976.

## Amazing Olympics

Nadia Comãneci made history at the 1976 Olympics in Montreal, when she scored the first perfect 10 ever given in a gymnastics competition, for her routine on the uneven bars.

## Trampolining

The newest gymnastics sport is trampolining, introduced in 2000. The competitors bounce up to 33 feet (10 m) high, doing somersaults, twists, and backflips to earn marks from the judges. Sequences of trampoline somersaults and twists have special names, including the rudolph, cat leap, and fliffi. The judges give high scores for style and technique and for landing accurately on the trampoline.

## Weightlifting

There are 15 weightlifting events for men and women, organized in different classes based on the bodyweight of the competitors. The weightlifters must hoist a barbell, a metal bar loaded with weighted disks on either end. More disks are gradually added to make the barbell heavier. There are two kinds of lifts. In a "clean and jerk," the weightlifter raises the barbell to his shoulders while squatting, then stands up and lifts the barbell overhead. In a "snatch" lift, the weightlifter starts the move standing, then lifts the barbell up. The referees judge if the lifts have been done correctly; otherwise they don't count.

Latvia's Viktors Scerbatihs wins bronze in the men's super-heavyweight weightlifting competition.

### Olympic Facts and Stats

Male Olympic gymnasts don't have music for their floor exercises, but women do.

Rope-climbing was once an Olympic gymnastics event. It was scored by the height the climbers achieved and for their climbing style.

Weightlifters wear special weightlifting shoes that help them to grip the floor as they lift.

In Paralympic powerlifting, the competitors lie down and push the barbell upward.

The Winter Olympics, held every four years, attracts the best winter sports athletes in the world. Categories include skiing, ice hockey, curling, luge, bobsled, and ice-skating.

Ski events include alpine (downhill) skiing, cross-country skiing, freestyle skiing, and snowboarding. Alpine skiers ski as fast as they can down a hillside course. Cross-country skiers trek over a countryside course. Freestyle skiing includes exciting mogul competitions, when skiers race down a bumpy track or perform tricks over the bumps (called moguls). Ski-cross and snowboard-cross are exciting high-speed races between four competitors, while the aerial skiing and snowboard half-pipe events produce breathtaking acrobatics that are scored by watching judges.

## Luge and Bobsled

The luge and bobsled competitions are the high-speed events of the Winter Olympics. Lugers lie on their backs on a sled, steering it by moving their body as

Hannah Teter of the United States competes in the snowboard womens' half-pipe, Vancouver, 2010.

they hurtle down an icy track at up to almost 95 mph (150 km/h) with no brakes. Bobsled teams of two or four jump into a bobsled shaped like a rocket, with brakes and steering pulleys, and race around a course at nearly 95 mph (150 km/h). The skeleton bobsledders lie on their stomachs on a sled that looks like a large tray with handles, reaching speeds of up to 85 mph (135 km/h) as they shoot down the track.

Shen Xue and Xao Honbo win gold for China in the pairs figure-skating competition in Vancouver, 2010.

## On the Ice

Indoor Winter Olympic events include curling, ice hockey, and ice-skating. Curling and ice hockey are both exciting competitions. Hockey requires bravery and quick reactions, while curling needs concentration to make accurate shots. As individuals or pairs, ice skaters perform to music and are scored by judges for technique and artistic merit.

### Amazing Olympics

The Winter Olympics and the Summer Olympics take place two years apart. The next Winter Olympics will be held in 2014, in Sochi, Russia.

### Olympic Facts and Stats

The Winter Paralympics take place immediately after the Winter Olympics, in the same venue. They include ice-sled hockey and wheelchair curling.

Lugers wear gloves fitted with sharp spikes 0.16 inches (4 mm) long, to help them push on the ice at the beginning of a run.

Bobsledders and lugers wear helmets like motor-racing drivers, along with tight-fitting aerodynamic suits.

Ski jumpers launch themselves from a high ramp, hitting speeds above 56 mph (90 km/h) as they reach the end of the ramp.

# GLOSSARY

**Barbell** A metal bar with weighted plates fitted on either end, for weightlifters to raise up.

**Biathlon** An event that combines a cross-country skiing race with a shooting competition.

**Bull's-eye** The center of a shooting or archery target. Hitting the bull's-eye scores the highest number of points.

**Compulsory round** A performance in which a competitor must do certain set moves.

**Coxswain** Someone who sits in the back of a rowboat facing the front, steering and keeping the oarsmen or women rowing together.

**Decathlon** An event for men that consists of ten different sports. Competitors build up a score as they take part in each one.

**Dressage** A series of very precise movements made by a horse.

**Equestrian events** Horseback riding competitions.

**Field events** Events that take place in the center of the main Olympic Stadium, such as throwing and jumping events.

**Freestyle** An event where competitors can perform their own unique routine.

**Halfpipe** A U-shaped track used for snowboarding performances.

**Heptathlon** An event for women that consists of seven sports.

**Hurdles** Jumps placed on the athletics running track, for hurdling and steeplechase events.

**IOC** International Olympic Committee, the organization that runs the Olympic Games.

**Judges** Experts who give scores to Olympic competitors in sports such as gymnastics and ice-dancing.

**Lanes** Separate routes for each competitor, marked on a track or in a swimming pool.

**Long-distance running** Races of 5,000 m or 10,000 m.

**Marathon** A long-distance running race that takes place through the streets of the host city during the Summer Olympics.

**Middle-distance running** Races of 800 m and 1,500 m.

**Modern pentathlon** An event that consists of five different sports.

**Mogul** A man-made bump on a snowy track.

**Olympian** Someone who has competed in the Olympics.

**Paralympics** Summer and Winter Olympic Games held every four years for disabled athletes.

**Performance-enhancing drugs** Drugs taken to make an athlete perform better (also called "doping").

**Pictogram** A picture symbol given to every Olympic sport.

**Red flag** Waved by a judge if a long jumper steps too far forward before jumping.

**Skeet** A shooting event, where competitors fire at clay disks shot into the air.

**Slalom** A course where a competitor must weave around poles or go through gates, used in skiing and canoeing.

**Sprinter** A fast runner who runs in short races of 100 m, 200 m, or 400 m.

**Steeplechase** A running race where athletes have to jump hurdles, some with water-filled ditches in front.

**Synchronized** Where a team performs exactly the same moves at the same time, such as in synchronized diving and swimming.

**Track events** Athletics events that are run around the track in the main Olympic stadium.

**Velodrome** Cycling arena.

**Youth Olympics** Summer and Winter Olympic Games held every four years for athletes who are between 14 and 18 years of age.

# LIST OF OLYMPIC EVENTS

## Summer Olympics

Aquatics (swimming pool sports)

Archery

Badminton

Basketball

Boxing

Canoeing

Cycling

Equestrian (horseback riding)

Fencing

Gymnastics

Handball

Hockey

Judo

Modern pentathlon

Rowing

Sailing

Shooting

Soccer

Table tennis

Tae kwon do

Tennis

Track and Field

Triathlon

Volleyball

Weightlifting

Wrestling

## Winter Olympics

Biathlon

Bobsled

Curling

Ice hockey

Luge

Skating

Skiing (alpine, cross-country)

## Summer Paralympics

Archery

Boccia

Cycling

Equestrian

Goalball

Judo

Powerlifting

Rowing

Sailing

Shooting

Soccer (5-a-side, 7-a-side)

Swimming

Table tennis

Track and field

Volleyball

Wheelchair basketball

Wheelchair fencing

Wheelchair rugby

Wheelchair tennis

## Winter Paralympics

Biathlon

Cross-country skiing

Ice-sled hockey

Skiing (alpine, cross-country)

Wheelchair curling

**Useful Olympic Websites**

www.olympic.org - The official web site of the Olympic Movement

www.teamusa.org - Official site for the U.S. Olympic Team

www.london2012.com - The official website of the London Summer Olympics 2012

www.paralympics.org - The official web site of the Paralympics

www.historyforkids.org/learn/greeks/games/olympics.htm - Find out about the history of the Ancient Greek Games

# INDEX